BOURBON MIXOLOGY

Bourbon Cocktails from the Craft Distillers Featured in the Book Small Brand America V

BY
STEVE AKLEY

Written and Published by:
Steve Akley

To Bourbon Mixologists Everywhere:

You never want to override the smooth taste of a great bourbon by mixing it in a cocktail unless you are making something special. These cocktails do it right!

Bourbon Mixology

Introduction by Steve Akley, Author

Craft distillers have found one of the vital ways to connect with everyone in their supply chain is through cocktail recipes. Employees are often the first to try different experiments with their brand. Distributors put together their own recipes to generate retail interest. Bartenders create unique concoctions which draw customers to these new offerings and showcase their bartending skills. Blogs are dedicated to individuals creating new drinks. Fans send in their ideas. Even the master distillers and the owners seem to enjoy the artistry of creating drinks.

Bourbon Mixology represents the best of these cocktails from the companies featured in **Small Brand America V: Special Bourbon Edition**. You are encouraged to seek out the brands highlighted here to incorporate into the recipes they have submitted. It gives you the true experience of sampling these cocktails.

No true tasting of a regional brand would be complete without a "neat" sampling to ensure the full impact of the difference between it and the megabrands produced in Kentucky. Still, there's a fun quotient to mixing up a recommended cocktail and seeing how those flavors meld with the other ingredients.

I suggest you mix up a favorite here, grab **Small Brand America V: Special Bourbon Edition** and read about the people and the stories behind the brands featured.

Cheers!

Table of Contents

Chapter 1
2bar Spirits

2960 4th Avenue South
Seattle, WA 98134
(206) 402-4340

2barspirits.com
info@2barspirits.com

Established
2010

Leadership
Nathan Kaiser, Owner

2bar Toddy
Cold day = hot drink.

Submitted by: 2bar Spirits

Serve in a stylized mug:
- ½ Cup hot water
- 2 oz 2bar Bourbon
- 1 oz Letterpress Limoncello
- Lemon peel
- Cinnamon stick
- Heat water with lemon peel and cinnamon stick in a saucepan until simmering
- Transfer to a mug and mix in the bourbon and limoncello

Maple Old Fashioned
A delicious twist on the grandfather of all cocktails.

Submitted by: 2bar Spirits

Mix and serve in a rocks glass:
- 2 oz 2bar Bourbon
- 1½ oz Sparkling water
- ½ oz Fresh squeezed orange juice
- ½ oz Maple syrup
- 1 Dash Angostura Bitters
- Mix orange juice, maple syrup, and bitters
- Add bourbon, a single ice cube, and top with sparkling water
- Garnish with an orange slice or zest

Chapter 2

10th Mountain Whiskey & Spirit Company

286 Bridge Street
Vail, CO 81657
(970) 470-4215

10thwhiskey.com
ryan@10thwhiskey.com or christian@10thwhiskey.com

Established
2014

Leadership
Christian Avignon & Ryan Thompson, Co-Founders

The Alpen Apple

Submitted by: Ian Tulk, Mixologist – 10th Mountain Whiskey & Spirit Co.

Serve in a martini glass:
- 2 oz 10th Mountain Whiskey & Spirit Company Bourbon
- 1 oz Cocchi Americano
- 1 oz Apple puree
- 1 oz Ginger lime shrub
- Mix ingredients and shake in a shaker with ice
- Strain
- Garnish with fresh apple crisp and serve

A Manhattan with Altitude

Submitted by: Ian Tulk, Mixologist – 10th Mountain Whiskey & Spirit Co.

Serve in a martini glass:
- 2 oz 10th Mountain Whiskey & Spirit Company Bourbon
- ½ oz 10th Mountain Alpenglow Cordial
- 1 oz Genepy Alpine Liqueur
- Splash Amarena Cherry Juice
- 4 dashes bitters
- Mix ingredients and shake in a shaker with ice
- Strain
- Garnish with fresh rosemary and lemon twist and serve

The Riva Ridge
The 10ᵗʰ Mountain twist on the Negroni

Submitted by: Ian Tulk, Mixologist – 10ᵗʰ Mountain Whiskey & Spirit Co.

Mix and serve in a rocks glass:
- 1 ½ oz 10ᵗʰ Mountain Whiskey & Spirit Company Bourbon
- 1 ½ oz Capilletti (Campari may be substituted)
- 1 ½ oz Fortified wine (suggested: Rainwater Madeira)
- Stir ingredients together in a rocks glass
- Add large orange zest
- Serve with one large ice cube

Smokey the Pear

Submitted by: Ian Tulk, Mixologist – 10th Mountain Whiskey & Spirit Co.

Mix and serve in a rocks:
- 2 oz Pine nut infused 10th Mountain Whiskey & Spirit Company Bourbon
- 1 oz Roasted clove pear puree
- 1 oz Ruby port
- 2 Smoked ice cubes
- Mix in a rocks glass
- Serve with shaved pear ribbons for garnish

The Chamonix

Submitted by: Ian Tulk, Mixologist – 10th Mountain Whiskey & Spirit Co.

Serve in a rocks glass:
- 2 oz Cardamom infused 10th Mountain Whiskey & Spirit Company Bourbon
- 1 oz Cointreau
- ¾ oz Lemon juice
- ½ oz Simple syrup
- ½ oz Egg white
- Mix ingredients and shake in a shaker with ice
- Strain ingredients and serve neat in a rocks glass with fresh sage

Chapter 3
Black Dirt Distillery

BLACKDIRTDISTILLERY.COM

Pine Island, NY
(845) 216-6900

blackdirtdistillery.com
info@blackdirtdistillery.com

Warwick Winery: 114 Little York Road, Warwick, NY 10990

Established
2012

Leadership
Jeremy Kidde & Jason Grizzanti, Co-Founders & Managing
Partners

Black Dirt® Manhattan

Submitted by: Black Dirt Distillery

Serve in a double rocks glass:
- 2 oz Black Dirt Bourbon
- 1 oz American Fruits sour cherry cordial
- ½ oz Grand Marnier
- 2 dashes Angostura Bitters
- Stir ingredients
- Serve over ice in a double rocks glass

Chapter 4
Coulter & Payne Farm Distillery

Shawnee Bend Farms
Union, MO 63084
(636) 395-7418

coulterandpaynefarmdistillery.com
info@coulterandpayne.com

Established
2011

Leadership
Chris Burnette, President, Owner and Head Distiller
Elise Burnette, Vice-President and Owner
William Uphouse, Distiller and Owner
Matt Schimmel, Distiller and Owner

Bourbon, Spice and Everything Nice

Here's a cocktail straight from the Coulter & Payne Farm Distillery's test kitchen. Sweet and warm, with hints of lemon, cinnamon, and cream, this cocktail is sure to make your holidays warm, cozy and fun.

Submitted by: Elise Burnette, Vice-President of Design, C&P

Serve in a rocks glass:
- 1 oz Coulter & Payne Small Batch Bourbon
- 1 oz Crop Circle Moonshine (or other traditional Appalachian corn whiskey)
- ½ oz Freshly squeezed lemon juice
- ½ oz Simple syrup
- 5 Dashes of Angostura Bitters
- Combine ingredients in a cocktail mixer
- Shake for 10 seconds
- Add one egg white and shake for an additional 15 seconds
- Add ice and shake one last time to finish
- Strain through a fine mesh strainer into a glass
- Garnish with white sparkling sugar sprinkles, serve and enjoy

Good Morning

Need a great way to wake up? Try this for an energizing way to start the day.

Submitted by: Amanda Snyder, Director of Retail Sales, C&P

 or

Serve in a coffee mug or your favorite glass:
- 1 Cup of any small batch, locally roasted, brewed coffee
- 1 ½ oz Coulter & Payne Small Batch Bourbon
- Pour into a glass over ice, stir, and serve

Manhattan on the Farm
Our Small Batch Bourbon & our Crop Circle Moonshine Corn Whiskey mesh together in a delightful, rustic, yet classic take on the Manhattan.

Submitted by: Chris Burnette, President, C&P

Prepare and serve in a rocks glass:
- 2 oz Coulter & Payne Small Batch Bourbon
- ½ oz Crop Circle Moonshine (or other traditional Appalachian corn whiskey)
- 1 oz Sweet vermouth
- 2 Dashes of bitters
- Combine all ingredients and stir
- Serve over ice with a cherry

Backroads Apprehension
Vanilla, caramel and butterscotch open the experience, married with the sweet and tart notes of apricot and a citrus nose.

Submitted by: Nicholas Crow, Sales Representative, C&P

Serve in a rocks glass:
- 2 oz Coulter & Payne Small Batch Bourbon
- 1 oz Apricot liqueur
- ¾ oz Sweet vermouth
- Combine all ingredients in a cocktail mixer
- Add ice and stir for 15 seconds
- Strain into glass
- Garnish with flamed orange oil and peel

A Dream in a Peach
Utilizing fresh ingredients to create a delightful, refreshing cocktail.

Submitted by: Anna Fox, Assistant Vice-President of Marketing, C&P

Prepare and serve in a rocks glass:
- 2 oz Coulter & Payne Small Batch Bourbon
- ½ Peach (fresh peeled and pitted)
- 1 tsp Sugar
- 2 Dashes Angostura Bitters
- 2 Cherries
- Place peach, 1 cherry, sugar and bitters in the bottom of a glass
- Muddle gently in the glass
- Add ice and bourbon
- Stir gently and garnish with a cherry and serve

The Bourbon Reforms
Originally created for the inaugural cocktail menu at the Mission Taco Joint in St. Louis. Corn flavors pair well with spice, pepper and citrus.

Submitted by: Joel Clark, Bar Manager, The Purple Martin (2800 Shenandoah Avenue, St. Louis, MO 63104 / *thepurplemartinstl.com*)

Prepare and serve in a rocks glass:
- 1 oz Coulter & Payne Small Batch Bourbon
- ½ oz Crop Circle Moonshine
- ½ oz Benedictine
- 1 oz Sweet vermouth
- 1 Pipette Bitterman's Hellfire Habanero Bitters
- Combine all ingredients in cocktail mixer
- Add ice, stir for 15 seconds and strain into glass
- Garnish with lemon oil and peel

Broad Side of the Barn

*Sweet and creamy corn flavors subdued by hints of orange and ginger,
finished with a balanced bitter note and citrus.*

Submitted by: Nicholas Crow, Sales Representative, C&P

Serve in a rocks glass:

- ¾ oz Coulter & Payne Small Batch Bourbon
- ¾ oz Crop Circle Moonshine (or other traditional Appalachian corn whiskey)
- ½ oz Ginger liqueur
- ½ oz Fresh lemon juice
- ½ oz Simple syrup
- 3 Dashes Angostura Bitters
- 1 Egg white
- Combine all ingredients into a cocktail mixer
- Shake without ice for 10 seconds
- Add ice and shake an additional 10 seconds
- Fine strain mixture into the glass
- Allow the head/froth to form and settle before creating a design using bitters and a cocktail straw
- Serve

Chapter 5
Dark Corner Distillery

241-B North Main Street
Greensville, SC 29601
(864) 631-1144

darkcornerdistillery.com
info@darkcornerdistillery.com

Established
2012

Leadership
Joe Fenten, Founder & President

Major's Nightcap

Submitted by: Whitney Vadeboncoeur, Dark Corner Distillery

Serve in a rocks glass:
- 1 ½ oz Lewis Redmond Carolina Bourbon
- 1 oz Orange juice
- ½ oz Amaretto
- ½ oz Lemon juice
- 1 tsp Maple syrup
- Combine ingredients in a shaker with ice
- Mix
- Strain over fresh ice into a rocks glass

The Prince

Submitted by: Whitney Vadeboncoeur, Dark Corner Distillery

Serve in a martini glass:
- 2 oz Lewis Redmond Carolina Bourbon
- 1 oz Club soda
- ½ oz Lemon juice
- 3 Thin pear slices
- 1 tbsp Honey
- 1 Dash of Angostura Bitters
- 1 Sage leaf
- First, make a honey syrup by combing equal parts honey and hot water
- In a shaker, muddle 2 thin slices of pear with honey syrup
- Top with ice
- Add bourbon, lemon juice and bitters
- Shake
- Strain into a martini glass
- Top with club soda and garnish with sage leaf and pear slice

Cider House Rules

Submitted by: Whitney Vadeboncoeur, Dark Corner Distillery

Serve in a martini glass:
- 2 oz Lewis Redmond Carolina Bourbon
- 2 oz Apple cider
- ½ oz Campari
- 3 Dashes of plum bitters
- 1 Apple slice
- In a shaker, mix ingredients with ice
- Shake
- Strain into a martini class
- Garnish with the apple slice

Buttered Bourbon Beer

Submitted by: James Willis, Greenville, South Carolina

Serve in a rocks glass:
- 1 ½ oz Lewis Redmond Carolina Bourbon
- 2 oz Cream soda
- 2 oz Pasteurized egg whites
- ½ oz Butterscotch moonshine
- 1 Pinch of white cane sugar
- 2 Dashes of vanilla extract
- In a shaker with ice, combine bourbon and moonshine
- Shake
- Strain into glass
- Top with chilled, cream soda
- In the same mixer, without ice, combine egg whites with extract and add the pinch of sugar
- Shake vigorously until the egg whites have foamed into a meringue
- Float the whipped meringue on top of the cocktail

Bourbon Tea-Time

Submitted by: Joe Fenten, Dark Corner Distillery

Serve in a rocks glass:

- 2 oz Lewis Redmond Carolina Bourbon
- 3 oz Unsweetened ice black tea
- ½ oz Triple sec
- 1 Mint sprig
- 1 Lemon wedge
- In a mixer, muddle lemon, mint sprig and bourbon
- Add ice
- Top with triple sec and black tea
- Shake
- Stain over fresh ice
- Garnish with a lemon wedge

Old Vanilla

Submitted by: Joe Fenten, Dark Corner Distillery

Mix and serve in a rocks glass:
- 2 oz Lewis Redmond Carolina Bourbon
- 2 Dashes orange bitters
- ¼ oz Simple syrup
- Vanilla bean (split)
- Orange zest
- In a rocks glass, muddle vanilla bean, orange zest, simple syrup and orange bitters
- Add bourbon and ice
- Stir
- Garnish with an orange zest

Bourbon Peach Smash

Submitted by: Joe Fenten, Dark Corner Distillery

Serve in a rocks glass:
- 2 oz Lewis Redmond Carolina Bourbon
- 1 oz Peach purée
- ½ oz Simple syrup
- 1 Peach slice
- 3 Mint leaves
- In a mixing glass, muddle the mint, simple syrup and lemon juice
- Add ice, bourbon and peach purée
- Shake
- Strain into an ice-filled rocks glass
- Garnish with peach slice

Redmond's Cherry Coke

Submitted by: Joe Fenten, Dark Corner Distillery

Mix and serve in a rocks glass:
- 2 oz Lewis Redmond Carolina Bourbon
- 2 oz Cola
- ½ oz Maraschino cherry liqueur
- Combine ingredients in a rocks glass over ice
- Stir
- Garnish with a cherry

Desperado

Submitted by: Whitney Vadeboncoeur, Dark Corner Distillery

Serve in a rocks glass:
- 1 oz Lewis Redmond Carolina Bourbon
- 1 oz Apple moonshine
- 2 oz Spicy ginger ale
- ½ oz Cognac
- Apple slice
- Combine bourbon, moonshine and cognac into a mixer and shake
- Strain over fresh ice
- Top with spicy ginger ale
- Garnish with an apple slice

Lewis Manhattan

Submitted by: Whitney Vadeboncoeur, Dark Corner Distillery

Serve in a martini glass:
- 2 oz Lewis Redmond Carolina Bourbon
- ½ oz Fernet branca
- 1 tsp Maple syrup
- Lemon twist
- In a shaker, combine ingredients with ice
- Stir with cocktail spoon
- Strain into martini glass
- Garnish with a lemon twist

Chapter 6
Grand Traverse Distillery

781 Industrial Circle Drive, Suite 5
Traverse City, MI 49686
(231) 947-8635

grandtraversedistillery.com
info@grandtraversedistillery.com

Established
2005

Leadership
Kent Rabish, Owner

Northern Michigan Manhattan

Submitted by: Grand Traverse Distillery

Serve in a rocks glass:
- 2 oz Grand Traverse Distillery Straight Bourbon Whiskey
- 1 oz Pine syrup (recipe below)
- ¼ oz Maple syrup
- 2 Dashes bitters, preferably house made
- 1 Bourbon soaked maraschino cherry skewered on an orange twist
- Fill a mixing glass with ice
- Add the bourbon, pine syrup, maple syrup and bitters
- Stir well with a proper cocktail spoon
- Strain into a chilled rocks glass and garnish with the cherry and twist

Pine Syrup Recipe
- 2 Cups fresh pine or spruce needles (off of the branch for freshness)
- 6 Cups of water
- 1 Cup of sugar (cane, brown, turbinado, etc.)
- Pick the needles off of the branch and rinse
- Chop the branch into small pieces and smash with a mallet to release oils
- In a medium saucepan, combine the needles, branch pieces and water
- Bring to a simmer and cook until the liquid is reduced to about 1 cup
- Stir in the sugar and dissolve completely and remove from the heat to cool

Pine Syrup Recipe (cont.)
- Once cooled completely, puree the mixture in a blender for 1 minute
- Strain into a jar and keep refrigerated for up to one month

Chapter 7
Heritage Distilling Co.

3207 57th Street Court NW
Gig Harbor, WA 98335
(253) 509-0008

heritagedistilling.com
info@heritagedistilling.com

Established
2011

Leadership
Jennifer Stiefel, Founder and President and Justin Stiefel, Founder, CEO & Master Distiller

Bourbon Cookie Dough Milkshake

Submitted by: Natalie Migliarini at *beautifulbooze.com*

Serve in a double rocks glass:
- 2 oz Heritage Distilling Elk Rider Bourbon
- 4 Scoops of cookie dough ice cream
- ¼ Cup of milk
- 1 tsp Chocolate sauce for garnish
- 1 tbsp Chocolate curls for garnish
- In a blender, combine ice cream, milk and bourbon
- Blend until desired consistency (more ice cream if it is too thin / more milk if it is too thick)
- Pour blended mixture into serving glass
- Top with chocolate sauce drizzle and garnish with chocolate curls

Black Beauty

Submitted by: Jessica Torres, *onemartini.com*

Serve in a double rocks glass:
- 2 oz Heritage Distilling Elk Rider Bourbon
- 8 Blackberries
- ¾ oz Tarragon simple syrup (directions below)
- 1 oz Fresh squeezed lemon juice
- 1 Dash Angostura Bitters
- Soda water
- 1 Lemon wheel, 1 sprig of tarragon and 1 blackberry (garnish)
- To make tarragon simple syrup: Combine ½ cup raw sugar and ½ cup water in a small saucepan over a medium heat. Stir in to dissolve the sugar. Once the sugar is dissolved, add 2 sprigs of tarragon, turn the heat to low and let simmer for 5 minutes. Remove the pot from heat and let cool completely. Remove the sprigs of tarragon and transfer the syrup to a glass bottle and refrigerate until ready to use.
- Add blackberries, tarragon simple syrup and lemon juice to a cocktail shaker and muddle
- Add bourbon and bitters and fill shaker with ice
- Shake and double strain into a rocks glass filled with ice
- Top with soda water, stir and garnish with lemon wheel, tarragon and blackberry

Mason Dixon

Submitted by: Heritage Distilling Co.

  or

Serve in a rocks or coupe glass:
- 2 oz Heritage Distilling Elk Rider Bourbon
- ½ oz Heritage Distilling Company Peach Vodka
- Shake and serve over ice with a fresh peach wedge in a rocks glass or with a fresh peach slice in a coupe

Chapter 8
Mississippi River Distilling Company

303 N. Cody Road
LeClaire, IA 52753
(563) 484-4342

mrdistilling.com
info@mrdistilling.com

Established
2010

Leadership
Ryan and Garrett Burchett, Co-Owners

Bourbon Cream Liqueur

Submitted by: Mississippi River Distilling Company

Serve in an old fashioned glass:
- 1 ½ Cups Cody Road Bourbon
- 2 Eggs, well beaten
- 1 tsp Vanilla
- 14 oz Can of sweetened condensed milk
- 2 tbsp Hershey's Syrup
- 1 tsp Almond extract
- Heat milk and eggs until 180 degrees (DO NOT BOIL!)
- Strain the mixture (may need to do more than once) and cool
- Add vanilla, sweetened condensed milk, Hershey's Syrup, almond extract and bourbon
- Mix well and refrigerate
- Serve with ice in an old fashioned glass

Cody's Mint Julep

Submitted by: Mississippi River Distilling Company

Serve in a highball glass:
- 3 oz Cody Road Bourbon
- 3 – 5 Fresh mint leaves
- 2 tbsp Mint syrup (see recipe below)
- 1 Fresh mint sprig
- Place mint leaves and syrup in a chilled glass and muddle
- Pack cup tightly with crushed ice
- Add bourbon and a mint sprig and serve

Mint Syrup Recipe
- Need 1 ½ cups sugar and 15 – 20 fresh mint sprigs
- Boil 1 ½ cups sugar and 1 ½ cups water 2 to 3 minutes or until sugar dissolves
- Remove from heat, add 15 to 20 fresh mint sprigs and cool
- Cover and chill for 24 hours
- Strain syrup and discard solids

Bourbon Ginger Snap

Submitted by: Mississippi River Distilling Company

Serve in a cocktail glass:
- 1 Liter Cody Road Bourbon
- 1 Cup fresh lemon juice
- 1 Cup honey
- 1 Three inch piece of fresh ginger (peeled and sliced)
- 6 Cups fresh orange juice
- 4 Cups pear nectar
- 2 Lemons (thinly sliced)
- Create a lemon syrup in a large saucepan by combining 2 quarts of water, fresh lemon juice, honey and ginger; bring to a boil
- Reduce heat and simmer for 5 minutes
- Strain into a large bowl and let cool
- Add the orange juice, pear nectar, bourbon and lemons into the lemon syrup
- Serve over ice

Candied Pecan Bourbon

Submitted by: Mississippi River Distilling Company

Serve in a cocktail glass:
- 2 oz Cody Road Bourbon
- ½ Orange (juiced)
- 1 tbsp Pecan simple syrup (recipe below)
- 2 Dashes Peychaud's Bitters
- Mix over ice, stir, and serve

Pecan Simple Syrup Recipe
- 1 Cup sugar
- 1 Cup water
- ¼ Cup crushed pecans
- Combine water, pecans and sugar
- Heat until sugar is dissolved
- Let cool for a couple of hours
- Strain out the pecans keep the syrup in the refrigerator

Steeplechase

Submitted by: Mississippi River Distilling Company

Serve in a highball glass:
- 2 oz Cody Road Bourbon
- 3 – 4 Mint leaves
- ¼ oz Blackberry brandy
- ¼ oz Orange curacao liqueur
- 2 Dashes Angostura Bitters
- 2 oz Fresh orange juice
- Muddle the mint leaves with the curacao and brandy in the bottom of a mixing glass
- Add all other ingredients, shake well and strain into an old-fashioned glass
- Garnish with a sprig of mint and serve

Anchors Away

Submitted by: Mississippi River Distilling Company

Serve in a highball glass:
- 1 oz Cody Road Bourbon
- 2 tsp Triple sec
- 2 tsp Peach brandy
- 2 tsp Maraschino cherry liqueur
- 2 tbsp Heavy cream
- Several drops of maraschino cherry juice
- Mix with ice in a shaker
- Serve a highball glass with ice

Straw-Bourbon Lemonade

Submitted by: Mississippi River Distilling Company

Mix and serve in a rocks glass:
- 2 oz Cody Road Bourbon
- 1 tsp Strawberry daiquiri mix
- 1 Slice lemon
- ½ tsp Maple syrup
- 1 Dash cinnamon
- Club soda
- Mix first five ingredients in a rocks glass over ice
- Top with club soda to taste and serve

Hot Buttered Cody

Submitted by: Mississippi River Distilling Company

Mix and serve in a stylized mug:

- 2 ½ oz Cody Road Bourbon
- 6 oz Apple cider
- 1 tsp Brown sugar
- 1 tsp Butter
- 1 Cinnamon stick (or pinch of cinnamon)
- Dash of nutmeg
- Heat bourbon, brown sugar, butter and apple cider in a saucepan (do not heat long enough to burn off bourbon)
- Pour into a warm mug
- Add cinnamon stick (or pinch of cinnamon) and dash of nutmeg
- Enjoy!

Cody's Punch
Be careful... a little goes a long way with this one!

Submitted by: Mississippi River Distilling Company

Serve in a rocks glass:
- 375 ml (half a bottle) Cody Road Bourbon
- 6 Cans light beer
- 12 oz (1 can) Frozen lemonade concentrate
- Mix ingredients in a one gallon pitcher
- Add ice
- Stir and serve

Note: You can tame it down a bit by adding 12 oz of water

Mississippi Tea

Submitted by: Mississippi River Distilling Company

Serve in a Collins glass:
- 1 oz Cody Road Bourbon
- 5 ½ oz Sweetened ice tea
- 2 oz 7-Up
- Dash of lemon juice
- Pour the bourbon into a Collins glass filled with ice cubes
- Add lemon juice
- Fill ¾ of the way with sweetened ice tea
- Top with 7-Up
- Stir and serve

Chapter 9
New Holland Artisan Spirits

66 East 8th Street
New Holland, MI 49423
(616) 355-6422

newhollandbrew.com
info@newhollandbrew.com

Established
1996

Leadership
Brett VanderKamp, Co-Founder & President

A Michigander's Old Fashioned
Michigan reformulates the Old Fashioned.

Submitted by: Adam Dickerson, New Holland Artisan Spirits

Serve in a rocks glass:
- 2 oz New Holland Artisan Spirits Beer Barrel Bourbon
- ¼ oz Brown sugar simple syrup
- 2 Dashes apple bitters
- Stir all ingredients and pour into a rocks glass
- Rim glass and garnish with orange peel

Maddalena

Submitted by: Adam Dickerson, New Holland Artisan Spirits

Serve in a coupe glass:
- 1 ½ oz New Holland Artisan Spirits Beer Barrel Bourbon
- ½ oz Luxardo
- ¼ oz Cynar
- 2 Dashes apple bitters
- Stir all ingredients and pour into coupe glass
- Rim glass with orange peel and garnish with orange peel and cherry

Bukowski

Submitted by: Rich Blair, New Holland Artisan Spirits

Serve in a highball glass:
- 1 oz New Artisan Spirits Beer Barrel Bourbon
- 1 oz Ginger liqueur
- 1 oz Vanilla liqueur
- 7 oz Poet Oatmeal Stout
- Shake first three ingredients, strain into chilled highball glass and top with beer

Pussycat

Submitted by: Rich Blair, New Holland Artisan Spirits

Serve in a coupe glass:
- 1 1/2 oz New Artisan Spirits Beer Barrel Bourbon
- 1/2 oz Campari
- 1/2 oz Clockwork Orange Liqueur
- 1/2 oz Grapefruit juice
- Shake all ingredients and strain into chilled coupe glass

Velvet Elvis

Submitted by: Rich Blair, New Holland Artisan Spirits

Serve in a coupe glass:
- 2 oz New Artisian Spirits Beer Barrel Bourbon
- 1/2 oz Falernum
- 2 dashes Peychaud's Bitters
- Stir all ingredients and strain into chilled coupe glass

Chapter 10
Oregon Spirit Distillers

740 NE 1st Street
Bend, OR 97701
(541) 382-0002

oregonspiritdistillers.com
info@oregonspiritdistillers.com

Established
2009

Leadership
Kathy & Brad Irwin, Owners

Sinful C.W.

Try this cranberry bourbon cocktail recipe for the holiday season. It's a festive drink reminiscent of fall. The winter spices add a nice touch with a slight effervescence.

Submitted by: Buck Bales, D & D Bar and Grill (927 NW Bond St Bend, OR 97701

or

Serve in a coupe or martini glass:
- 2 oz C.W. Irwin Bourbon
- ½ oz Brown sugar simple syrup
- 2 Whole cloves
- 1 oz Cranberry juice
- Hard cider
- Cranberries for garnish
- Fill shaker with ice
- Add bourbon, cranberry juice, simple syrup and whole cloves
- Shake
- Strain into martini or couple glass and then top off with hard cider
- Garnish with fresh or frozen whole cranberries

Sinful C.W.

Submitted by: Nicole Rushton

Serve in a lowball glass:
- 2 oz C.W. Irwin Bourbon
- 2 oz Grapefruit juice
- 2 Dashes of grapefruit bitters
- Splash of simple syrup
- 4 – 6 Basil leaves
- 1 Basil sprig for garnish
- Begin by giving basil a light muddle in shaker tin
- Add ice and remaining ingredients
- Shake and strain into a lowball glass filled with ice
- Garnish with a sprig of fresh basil

C.W. Irwin Reviver

Submitted by: Nicole Rushton

Serve in a coupe glass:
- 1 oz C.W. Irwin Bourbon
- ¾ oz Lillet Blanc
- ¾ oz Cointreau
- ½ oz Lemon juice
- Mint sprig (for garnish)
- Fill cocktail shaker with ice
- Add C.W. Irwin Bourbon, Cointreau, Lillet Blanc and lemon juice
- Shake until well chilled (about 15 seconds)
- Strain into a chilled coupe and garnish with a mint sprig

Chapter 11
Syntax Spirits

625 3rd Street, Unit C
Greely, CO 80631
(970) 352-5466

syntaxspirits.com
info@syntaxspirits.com

Established
2010

Leadership
Heather Bean, Co-Founder

Better than Sex
Your mileage may vary, but we think it's pretty darn good.

Submitted by: Syntax Spirits

Mix and serve in a 12 oz glass:
- 1 ½ oz Syntax Spirits Bourbon
- ½ oz Syntax Spirits Devious Vanilla Vodka
- Splash of natural orange bitters (if available)
- Top with fresh-squeezed orange juice
- Garnish with orange zest, orange slice, or fresh cherry

Colorado Mule
Northern Colorado may not be Moscow, but right now it feels that way.

Submitted by: Syntax Spirits

 or

Mix and serve in a 12 oz. copper mug or rocks glass:
- 2 oz Syntax Spirits Bourbon
- Splash of roasted-ginger infused vodka (if available)
- Splash of natural lime bitters (if available)
- Juice of 1 small fresh lime or half of a large one
- Top with ginger beer or strong ginger ale
- Garnish with lime slice

Chapter 12
Woodstone Creek Winery & Distillery

WOODSTONE CREEK
ARTISAN WINERY & DISTILLERY

4712 Vine Street
Cincinnati, OH 45217

woodstonecreek.com
woodstonecreek@yahoo.com

Established
1997

Leadership
Don Outterson, Owner

Woodstone Creek Blends
These are recommended blends we offer at the distillery.

Submitted by: Woodstone Creek Artisan Winery & Distillery

 or

Mix and serve in a shot glass or a rocks glass:
- 50/50 split of Woodstone Creek 5-Grain Bourbon and a fortified wine product
- This can be split in a shot glass or in a rock glass with ice
- Woodstone recommends the following four fortified products for these cocktails:
    - Woodstone Creek Legacy Brandy Fortified Mead
    - Woodstone Creek Crowne Amber Brandy Fortified Spiced Mead
    - Woodstone Creek Laureate Ohio Red Wine Port
    - Woodstone Creek Ambiance Ohio White Wine Port

Woodstone Manhattan
This requires some planning but makes for an awesome drink!

Submitted by: Daniel Souder, Restaurant Manager (The Presidents Room – The Phoenx, 812 Race Street, Cincinnati, OH 45202 / souderd@thephx.com)

Serve in a coupe glass:
Drink Prep
- 375 mL Woodstone Ridge Runner 5-Grain White Bourbon
- 375 mL Dolin Blanc
- 6 Dashes Regan's Orange Bitters
- 6 Dashes Fee Brothers Old-Fashioned Bitters
- Combine in a nonreactive (glass is best) bottle with 2 honeycomb barrel stave inserts
- Let sit for 4-6 weeks, until desired oak influence

Drink Build
- 3 oz Aged whiskey-vermouth from batch
- 2 Solid dashes Fee Brothers Old-Fashioned Bitters
- Add to mixing glass with ice
- Stir 20 - 30 rotations for desired dilution
- Strain into 8 oz coupe
- Garnish with orange twist

Woodstone Creek Manhattan

Any drink involving fire always creates a fun presentation!

Submitted by: Benjamin Newby of Obscura (645 Walnut Street, Cincinnati, OH 45202 / *obscuracincinnati.com*)

Serve in a snifter:

- 2 ½ oz Woodstone Creek 5-Grain Bourbon
- 1 oz Woodstone Creek Laureate Ohio Port
- 3 Dashes Peychauds Bitters
- Stirred and strained into 8 ½ oz flask
- Smoke the flask with hickory wood using a culinary smoking gun
- Chill overnight
- Serve in smoking snifter with flamed orange garnish

To recreate the Obscura presentation place the snifter upside down on a wooden board. Fill glass with hickory smoke. To present, lift the glass and waft the smoke around. Put the snifter glass the correct way up, pour cocktail from flask and finish with a flamed orange because when there is smoke there is always fire.

Bonus Chapter
Author Steve Akley Shares A Few Recipes

steveakley.com
info@steveakley.com

Bourbon Slush

Literally served at every family get-together when I was growing up.

Submitted by: Steve Akley (via Sandy, his mom)

Serve in a rocks glass:
- 1 Can orange juice concentrate
- 1 Can lemonade concentrate
- 1 Can* plus 4 tsp. instant ice tea
- 1 Can* of any one of the **Small Brand America** featured bourbons
- Mix together and freeze overnight

*Can = Using one of the concentrate cans as a unit of measurement

Ingredients will freeze together in a slush-like consistency. Spoon into a rocks glass and enjoy.

Windmill Winter Wine

*This recipe was recently featured in **Entertainment Weekly** as a cocktail to enjoy while watching the movie **It's a Wonderful Life** (Clarence orders mulled wine at the bar). Louise Owens graciously allowed me to reprint it here.*

Submitted by: Louise Owens, "Queen of All Things Divine Between NY & LA", Windmill Lounge (5320 Maple Avenue, Dallas, TX 75235 / *windmill-lounge.com*)

Serve in a punch glass:
- 1 Bottle of dry red wine
- 1 Cup bourbon
- ½ Cup raisins
- 2 Cinnamon sticks
- 8 Whole cloves
- 1 Orange, halved
- 1 Slice fresh ginger ¼" thick
- Pour wine and bourbon into a slow cooker
- Place other ingredients into cheesecloth and tie closed, then add to the slow cooker
- Heat for 30 – 45 minutes (do not boil)
- Ladle into glass mugs
- Garnish with fresh citrus or dried fruits

Serves 8

Author's Notes/Resources

One of the greatest aspects about writing these books is meeting all of the great people behind the brands. Their personal stories, along with the stories of their businesses, continue to offer fascinating insight about owning a small brand in America today. Of course, writing about a subject as fun as bourbon doesn't hurt either!

I encourage you to learn more about these individuals and their businesses. To make your job a little easier, here's a recap of the websites for each:

2bar Spirits – *2barspirits.com*

10th Mountain Whiskey & Spirit Co. – *10thwhiskey.com*

Black Dirt Distillery – *blackdirtdistillery.com*

Coulter & Payne Farm Distillery – *coulterandpaynefarmdistillery.com*

Dark Corner Distillery – *darkcornerdistillery.com*

Grand Traverse Distillery – *grandtraversedistillery.com*

Heritage Distilling Co. – *heritagedistilling.com*

Mississippi River Distilling – *mrdistilling.com*

New Holland Artisan Spirits – *newhollandbrew.com*

Oregon Spirit Distillers – *oregonspiritdistillers.com*

Syntax Spirits – *syntaxspirits.com*

Woodstone Creek – *woodstonecreek.com*

Small Brand America V
Special Bourbon Edition

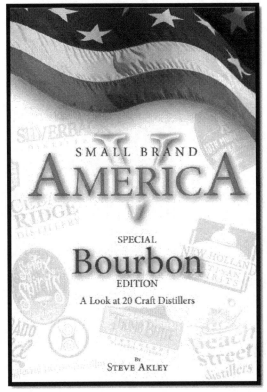

In **Small Brand America V**, author Steve Akley explores small companies making a name for themselves with a truly American original: bourbon. Each has a little bit of a different take on making America's favorite distilled spirit and a compelling story. Inevitably, you will find yourself wanting to learn more about the companies and a desire to try their product(s).

The Importance of Online Reviews

Reviews generate interest and create a buzz about the work of an author. Plus, your feedback is the only way an author knows if you enjoyed their work. Please take the time to review **Bourbon Mixology**! Steve would love to know what you think!

Photo Credits

All photographs in the sections of each business featured have been utilized with permission from the respective companies with the following exceptions:

2bar Spirits
Sasha Swerdorf (*tendingtable.com*) – 2bar Toddy and Maple Old Fashioned

Heritage Distilling Company
Natalie Migliarini (*beautifulbooze.com*) – Bourbon Cookie Dough Milkshake

Jessica Torres (*onemartini.com*) – Black Beauty

Woodstone Creek Artisan Winery & Distillery
Cincinnati Magazine – Woodstone Bourbon Bottle

Benjamin Newby, Obscura (*obscuracincinnati.com*) – Woodstone Creek Manhattan

Special Thanks

To my mom, Sandy Akley, and my wife Amy Akley, for their help in editing this book.

Thanks to my daughter Cat for just being herself.

Hats off to Mark Hansen (*mappersmark@gmail.com*) for the great cover design. He's the greatest graphic artist you will ever find!

The following individuals from the featured companies not only couldn't have been nicer, without their help this book would not have been possible:

Heather Bean, Syntax Spirits

Brenda at *tnwhiskeychicks.com*

Chris Burnette, Coulter & Payne Farm Distillery

Ryan Burchett, Mississippi River Distilling Company

Joe Fenten, Dark Corner Distillery

Tim Grovenburg, Dark Corner Distillery

Emily Haines, New Holland Artisan Spirits

Hannah Hanley, Heritage Distilling Co.

Kathy & Brad Irwin, Oregon Spirit Distillers

Jeremy Kidde, Black Dirt Distillery

Nathan Kaiser, 2bar Spirits

Natalie Migliarini, *beautifulbooze.com*

Benjamin Newby, Obscura (*obscuracincinnati.com*)

Don & Linda Outterson, Woodstone Creek Winery and Distillery

Louise Owens (Queen of All Things Divine Between NY and LA), Windmill Lounge (*windmill-lounge.com*/Dallas,TX)

Justin Stiefel, Heritage Distilling Co.

Ryan Thompason, 10th Mountain Whiskey & Spirit Company

Jessica Torres, *onemartini.com*

Brett VanderKamp, New Holland Artisan Spirits

Lastly, lots of love for my father, Larry Akley. He's always with us in spirit.

In Loving Memory of Larry Akley
1942 – 2012

Dad's badge photo compliments of Kelly Brooks (thanks sis!)

Love A Cat Charity – Honolulu, Hawai'i

Steve Akley proudly supports the mission of Love A Cat Charity with a donation from the proceeds of the sale of all of his books.

Mission Statement

Love A Cat Charity's mission is to help end euthanasia of unwanted cats by caring for feral and abandoned felines, spaying or neutering them and, when appropriate, adopting them out. Love A Cat Charity emphasizes the use of Trap-Neuter-Return (TNR) technique to humanely control feral cat populations. Cats are humanely trapped, spayed or neutered and returned to their outdoor homes. TNR improves the cats' health and stabilizes the colony while allowing them to live out their lives outdoors. No new kittens are born and the cats no longer experience the stresses of mating and pregnancy.

Support of Love A Cat Charity in Honolulu, HI, helps cats like this sweet kitty

Love A Cat Charity
P.O. Box 11753
Honolulu, HI 96828
loveacatcharity.org

About the Author

Steve Akley is a lifelong St. Louis resident. Steve's approach to his writing is very simple. He knows his passion for writing comes from topics he enjoys so he sticks to what he knows best.

And yes… he likes bourbon:

Sign up for his newsletter, or check out his latest work, on his website: steveakley.com. Steve also maintains an author's page on Amazon.com. Just search his name on the site.

He can be reached via email: info@steveakley.com.

Find Steve on Social Media

@steveakley WORDPRESS & Steve Akley

Small Brand America – The Series

This "Special Bourbon Edition" is the fifth edition and sixth overall book in Steve's **Small Brand America** series.

All Small Brand America books chronicle the stories of small companies taking on much larger competitors. You learn about the brands and the people behind them.

Here's a look at all of the books:

Small Brand America I & II each focus on 25 companies in the grocery business. Additionally, **Small Brand America I** has a companion piece; a cookbook featuring recipes from the companies highlighted in the book.

 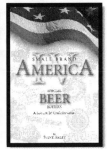

Small Brand America III & IV are each special editions. **SBA III** features companies all based in Hawaii and **SBA IV** features craft brewers.

Also by Steve Akley

Leo the Coffee Drinking Cat Series

A children's series featuring the adventures of a coffee drinking cat named Leo and his family.

Coffeehouse Jazz

Designed to assist you in building the ultimate playlists of jazz music. At 99¢, they cost less than the price of downloading a single song!

Steve Akley's Commuter Series

Short stories available for Kindle, iBooks and other electronic retailers

Only $1.49 each!

Be sure to check out Steve's website:

www.steveakley.com